FREE

Compliments of
FRIENDS OF THE
NC - HC LIBRARY

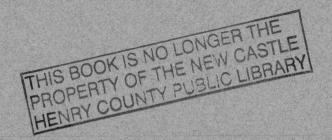

KOMODO DRAGONS

Giant Lizards of Indonesia

By James Martin

Illustrated with photographs
by the author

Reading consultant:

John Manning, Professor of Reading, University of Minnesota

Capstone Press

MINNEAPOLIS

J597.95
MART

Capstone Press • 2440 Fernbrook Lane • Minneapolis, MN 55447

Editorial Director   John Coughlan
Managing Editor   John Martin
Copy Editor   Gil Chandler

Library of Congress Cataloging-in-Publication Data

Martin, James, 1950-
    Komodo dragons : giant lizards of Indonesia / by James
    Martin.
        p. cm.
    Includes bibliographical references and index.
    ISBN 1-56065-238-1
    1. Komodo dragon--Juvenile literature. [1. Komodo
    dragon. 2. Lizards.] I. Title.
    QL666.L29M35   1995
    597.95--dc20   94-22822
                                                    CIP
                                                    AC

ISBN: 1-56065-238-1

99 98 97 96 95   8 7 6 5 4 3 2 1

Table of Contents

Facts about Komodo Dragons

Scientific Name: *Varanus komodoensis*

Description:

Length: While most adult dragons reach six feet, the largest on record was more than ten feet (three meters) long. The males are slightly larger than the females.

Weight: The average weight for a male is a little more than one hundred pounds (45 kilograms). The largest **specimens** exceed 300 pounds (136 kilograms). Some reach as much as 550 pounds (249 kilograms).

Physical Features: Komodo dragons have long necks. The tails are longer than the bodies in youngsters and shorter in adults. The teeth curve back and are **serrated**. The tongue is yellow and forked.

Color: Adult dragons are a dusty grey with spare flecks of color. Young dragons are almost black with bright yellow markings.

Habits: Dragons sleep at night and hunt during the day. They spend their nights in a den. During the day, they follow a well-worn route looking for food. Adult dragons will eat young dragons if given the chance. Some dragons swim to nearby islands to hunt.

Food: Dragons will eat any meat. They seem to prefer rotting flesh, but will eat live meat, too.

Reproduction: Mating usually occurs from July through September. The female will lay 20-30 eggs. Baby dragons must take care of themselves.

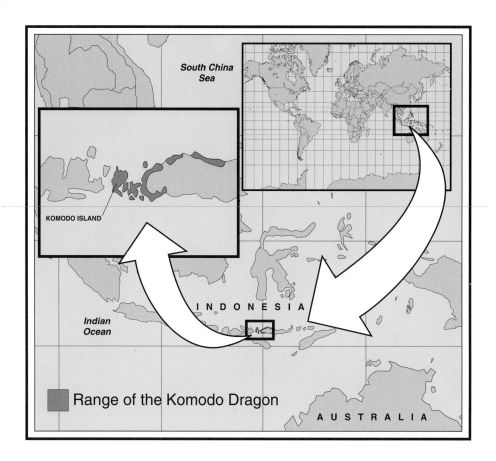

Life span: No one knows how long dragons live in the wild.

Range: The dragons roam over Komodo and the neighboring islands of Rincha and Padar. They also inhabit the western tip of the island of Flores.

Habitat: The islands where the dragons live are grasslands. Forests line the creeks and palm trees dot the hillsides. The temperature is always hot. There is no winter or summer, only a rainy season and a dry season.

Chapter 1

Killers with Bad Breath

Monsters walk on the island of Komodo, in Indonesia. They sneak through the island's tall grasses, making a rustling noise. From time to time, a long, ugly head rises above the grass. A yellow forked tongue flickers, as the monster tests the air for the smell of flesh.

The Largest Lizards in the World

The monsters are Komodo dragons, the largest lizards in the world. Although they are a type of **monitor** lizard, no other monitor is

With a flick of its forked tongue, a Komodo dragon smells the air for a whiff of its prey.

nearly as big. The largest Komodo dragons are more than ten feet (3 meters) long and weigh more than 300 pounds (136 kilograms).

Fast and Flesh-eating

Komodos can't run far, but they can outrun a human for a short distance. You wouldn't want one of these dragons to catch you. Their jaws can tear away huge chunks of flesh with a single bite. Like other lizards, they can unhinge their jaws and swallow pieces of food larger than their heads.

Legendary Beasts

People have always feared large animals. Those who live and work near the sea tell stories about sea monsters. Africans have told of giant man-beasts. Legends of fire-breathing dragons are common in Asia.

Many of these legends have some basis in fact. Giant squids fifty feet (16 meters) long, great white sharks, and deadly whales are true-life monsters of the sea. In the mists of the tropical forests, a gorilla looks like a big, hairy human. The Komodo dragon may be the source of the ancient Asian dragon myths.

The island of Komodo has given its name to the world's largest lizard.

Dragons with Bad Breath

These giant reptiles look like dragons. And they have true dragon breath. After they feed on rotting flesh, bits of the flesh rot in their teeth. **Bacteria** from the flesh lives in their mouths, making a sickening smell.

Mouth Bacteria that Kill

They're dangerous, too. Dragons often bite their prey just to injure it. After they cut a tendon or tear a muscle, the injured animal limps away. A bacterial **infection** from the dragon's mouth kills the animal in a day or two. The dragon, along with other dragons, tracks down the body by following the stench. For some reason, the Komodo dragon prefers aged meat.

Chapter 2
Finding and Eating Prey

Because of the Komodo's taste for rotting meat, scientists once thought dragons were **scavengers**–animals that live from the meat of dead bodies. But research proved that dragons are skilled hunters of live prey, too.

To hunt, a dragon slithers along its favorite path each day. It picks a hiding spot and waits for an unsuspecting animal to pass by. While waiting, its forked tongue flicks through the air. Like other lizards, the dragon uses its tongue to smell and to find its prey.

A Tongue for Smelling

The two forks of the Komodo's tongue smell by detecting **molecules** in the air. Since there are a greater number of molecules near the source of the smell, the fork that senses more molecules is closer to the prey. The dragon follows this fork to track down a victim.

When the dragon finds its prey, it charges in a cloud of dust. Its hips swivel, its tail wags, and its mouth draws open. During a charge, the reptile breathes heavily, making a sound like a machine gun.

Eating Prey

Dragons will eat almost anything, except plants. Wild pigs and deer are their usual fare. If they find a cobra, they will hold its head down with one foot and rip the snake apart as they eat it. Eggs are another favorite, especially the eggs of the **megapode** bird. The megapode builds large dirt mounds for its nest.

A gang of Komodo dragons feasts on the flesh of a helpless victim.

Dragons dig the eggs from the nest and swallow them whole.

Watching dragons eat is not very pleasant. Ten of them may feed at one time. Each animal has sharp, two-inch (5-centimeter) claws that tear the flesh. They breathe in deep rasps, as if they were clearing their throats. They sneeze frequently, blowing out the flies that gather in their nostrils.

Teeth Sharp as Needles

Their teeth, which are as sharp as needles, are curved to prevent prey from escaping. Small ridges on the backs of the teeth allow the dragon to tear away chunks of food. If the meat gets caught in the dragon's throat, it will **regurgitate** the flesh and try to swallow it again.

The razor-sharp claws of the Komodo dragon are ideal for holding and ripping the flesh of its prey.

While eating, their jaws snap open and shut, and their claws flash through the air. But dragons are built tough. Their scales contain hard bits of bone that protect them from serious injury.

Resting After a Meal

After a big meal–they can eat half of their weight at one sitting–the dragons flop on the ground and rest. **Drool** gathers around their mouths as they gaze into space.

Although they are good hunters, Komodo dragons would be no match for smart land **predators** like tigers or bears. Komodos are slow and have poor endurance. With little competition from other predators, they haven't developed faster or better ways of hunting. And they aren't very smart. Instead, they rely on their size and their great strength to survive.

A trail sign warns hikers of dangerous Komodo traffic.

Chapter 3

Mating and Reproduction

Female dragons prefer to mate with the largest males. There are fewer than 500 female Komodos in the world. Because they are much more rare than males, each female is very important to the survival of the species.

Courting

A **courting** male approaches a female carefully. He may scratch the back of her neck with his claws. This makes a clicking sound over the scaly skin. At first, the female will reject the male. The male may then bring a

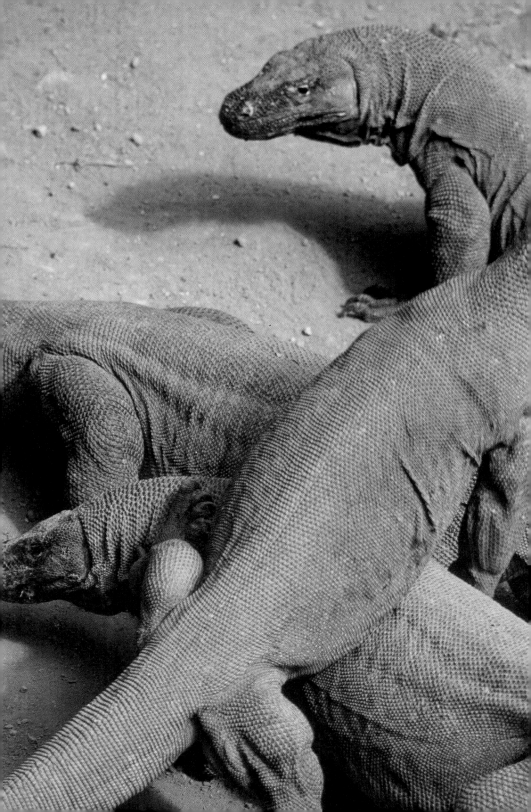

Baby Komodo dragons get no help from their parents. They must hunt and survive on their own.

present, such as the head of a dog, to the female.

In **captivity**, dragons lay 20 to 30 eggs at a time. But no Komodo dragon eggs have ever been found in the wild. Scientists who study dragons believe that the females must bury their eggs in a deep nest.

No Care from Parents

When babies dig themselves out of the nest, they receive no care from their parents. Young dragons must find their own food. They have to watch for dangerous predators like birds, snakes, and larger dragons.

Young Komodos climb high in the trees, where larger dragons can't attack them. As they grow larger, they begin visiting the large **kills**. They wait for the adults to leave before eating the scraps, so that they don't become part of the meal themselves.

Encounters with Humans

People are no match for a dragon, so the best defense is to stay as far away from a Komodo dragon as possible. Dragons can't run far. They run out of gas quickly. Most people can outrun them with a small head start.

In dragon country, large farm animals sometimes disappear. Komodos kill and eat 1,000-pound (450-kilogram) water buffalos as well as smaller goats, pigs, and chickens. Unlike most large predators, they will eat people, too.

Chapter 4

Komodo Dragons and Humans

Every few years Komodo dragons attack a human. In most cases a dragon was surprised and lashed out to defend itself.

But some dragons attack on their own. A bite can remove a human's entire muscle group and cause heavy bleeding. The dragon's mouth bacteria causes infection. The victim dies in a day or two.

In the 1970s a tourist wandered away from his friends. He might have sat down just to rest in the shade. He was never seen again. Searchers recovered only his camera.

Although the rest of the world thinks of dragons as legendary creatures, people living near Komodo know better. Years ago, the Sultan of Bima sent the worst criminals in his kingdom to Komodo. The terrified prisoners stayed on the beach, afraid to go into the forest where the dragons lay.

The **descendants** of these prisoners still live in Komodo's only village. The beach houses stand on stilts, partly to keep cool and partly to keep dragons out. Even today, dragons outnumber people on Komodo by more than two to one.

Digging Up the Dead

Dragons steal and eat livestock. And they dig up the dead. Komodo islanders put heavy rocks over the graves in their cemetery in order to prevent dragons from eating the bodies of their dead relatives.

The outside world didn't learn the truth about Komodo dragons until an expedition discovered them in 1910. These early explorers exaggerated the size and **ferocity** of the dragons. The first scientific study wasn't made until the 1960s.

Chapter 5

Komodo Dragons Past and Present

M onitor lizards are as ancient as the dinosaurs. Some of the ancient monitors have features like modern Komodo dragons.

Monitor lizards descend from **mosasaurs**, sea-going lizards that were as long as fifty feet (16 meters). The mosasaurs shared the seas with fifty-foot (16-meter) crocodiles, odd-looking sharks, and a dolphin-like dinosaur.

Indonesia is made up of thousands of islands—some of them tropical jungles, some of them grasslands.

But the mosasaur was the king of the seas. Its flippers sliced through the water at high speeds, and its long, sharp teeth tore into the flesh of its prey. Although it lived in the ocean, the mosasaur looked like a modern monitor lizard. Its long neck and skull could belong to a modern lizard, if we could imagine one of such great size.

The Komodo's Modern Home

Indonesia is an island nation between Australia and Southeast Asia. It includes part of Borneo and New Guinea. Its 10,000 islands–among them, Komodo Island–stretch across 3,000 miles (4,800 kilometers) of the Pacific Ocean.

Tropical jungles cover the western and eastern islands. Most of the central islands are dry grasslands, like southern California.

It's not wise to get too close to the Komodo, which is always on the lookout for a good meal.

Deadly spiders dangle from their webs on dangerous Komodo Island.

Orangutans and the rare Asian rhinoceros live in parts of Borneo and Sumatra. The Indonesian capital of Jakarta is on the island of Java, one of the most **densely** populated islands in the world. **Stone-Age** tribes live under the shadow of a 16,000-foot (5,000-meter) mountain in Irian Jaya, in western New Guinea.

Some of the most violent volcanic **eruptions** in history have occurred here. The Krakatoa explosion in 1883 killed thousands in **tidal waves**. Ash from the eruption darkened the skies of London, England–halfway around the world.

Komodo Island

Komodo Island in Indonesia is one of the most dangerous places in the world. Tropical **typhoons** rip trees from their roots. Strong currents swirl over the **reefs**, causing shipwrecks that leave **castaways** on the island.

The Dragons' Deadly Neighbors

During the rainy season, cobras and other poisonous snakes patrol the island's forests and grasslands. Deadly spiders hang from their webs, which they spin at face height above the ground. Poisonous **millipedes** march through the **underbrush**, their feet moving together like the oars on an ancient ship.

The Komodo dragons don't seem to mind. They fear nothing, except other dragons. In the past, humans have hunted dragons for research, for zoos, and for private collectors. But the Komodo's hard skin makes a poor leather, and nobody eats dragon meat. Today the Indonesian government protects the dragon and has made their home islands a national park.

Disease and Volcanoes

Aside from humans, disease and volcanoes are the biggest dangers for the dragon. If an epidemic broke loose, the dragons could become **extinct**. A volcanic eruption could cover the islands in hot ash, or start a tidal wave large enough to sweep many dragons out into the ocean.

Survival of the Komodo

To prevent such disasters, zoos all over the world are breeding the Komodos. For years, dragons have been born in Indonesian zoos.

The first successful births in the United States didn't happen until 1992. In that year, thirteen out of a **clutch** of twenty-six eggs hatched. The babies will go to several different zoos. An exchange program will increase the number of dragons in the world and help the species to survive.

Glossary

bacteria–tiny one-celled organisms

captivity–the condition of being held prisoner or under control

castaways–shipwrecked people

clutch–the eggs produced at a single laying or the chicks hatched from those eggs

courting–the act of wooing or seeking a mate

densely–thickly

descendant–a person or animal who is linked to an ancestor through one or more generations

drool–to let spit drip from the mouth

eruption–a sudden, often violent, shooting forth

extinction–no longer existing as a species

ferocity–fierceness

infection–the entry of microorganisms into the body

kill–an act of killing

megapode–a type of bird with very large feet

millipede–one of a group of animals having bodies with many segments, most segments having two pairs of legs

molecules–the smallest units that have the characteristic chemical and physical characterics of a compound

monitor–a name for a group of large lizards that live in Asia, Africa, or Australia

mosasaurs–a group of large lizards that roamed the earth during prehistoric times

orangutan–a large ape with long arms and reddish brown hair found on the islands of Borneo and Sumatra

predator–an animal that hunts other animals for food

reef–a strip of rock, sand, or coral that rises to the surface of a body of water

regurgitate–to vomit, to spit up partially digested food

scavenger–an animal that feeds on the remains of dead animals

serrated–with an edge that has notches or teeth

specimen–a sample

Stone-Age–from the earliest known period in human history, when stone tools and weapons were used

tidal wave–an unusually high level of water along a seacoast, caused by a storm or earthquake, or by a combination of wind and tide

typhoon–a tropical rainstorm in the western Pacific Ocean

underbrush–small trees and shrubs growing thickly beneath taller trees

To Learn More

Hopf, Alice L. *The Biography of a Komodo Dragon.* New York: Putnam, 1981.

Lutz, Dick and Marie Lutz. *Komodo, The Living Dragon.* Salem, OR: DIMI Press, 1991.

Schafer, Susan. *The Komodo Dragon.* New York: Dillon, 1992.

Jacobs, Judy. *Indonesia: A Nation of Islands.* New York: Dillon, 1990.

McNair, Sylvia. *Indonesia.* Chicago: Childrens Press, 1993.

Index